On and Off

T0020334

Saving Resources and Money

The light is **on.**

The light is **off.**

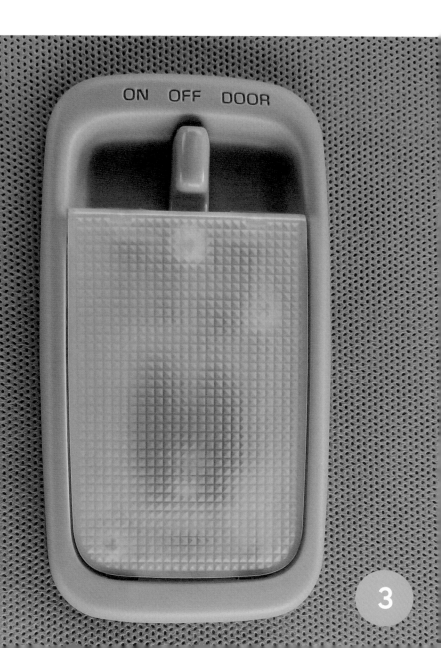

3

The lamp is on.

The lamp is off.

The street lights are on.

The street lights are off.

The car lights are on.

The car lights are off.

The torch light is on.

The torch light is off.

The party lights are on.

The party lights are off.

The garden light is on.

The garden light is off.

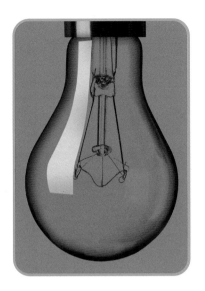

on